DATE DUE		

SUPREME COURT CASES

THROUGH PRIMARY SOURCES™

Miranda V. Arizona

The Rights of the Accused

Liz Sonneborn

rosen central
Primary Source™

The Rosen Publishing Group, Inc. New York

Published in 2004 by The Rosen Publishing Group, Inc.
29 East 21st Street, New York, NY 10010

Unless otherwise attributed, all quotes in this book are excerpted from court transcripts.

Library of Congress Cataloging-in-Publication Data

Sonneborn, Liz.
Miranda v. Arizona / by Liz Sonneborn.—1st ed.
    p. cm. — (Supreme Court cases through primary sources)
Includes bibliographical references and index.
ISBN 0-8239-4010-1 (library binding)
1. Miranda, Ernesto—Trials, litigation, etc. 2. Right to counsel—United States. 3. Confession (Law)—United States. 4. Police questioning—United States. I. Title: Miranda versus Arizona. II. Title. III. Series.
KF224.M54 S66 2004
345.73'056—dc21

2002154575

Manufactured in the United States of America

Contents

Introduction

A criminal runs down a dark street with a policeman close on his heels. The officer dives at the suspect, tackles him, then pulls out a pair of handcuffs and slaps them around the suspect's wrists. Still out of breath, the policeman recites the following words: "You have the right to remain silent. Anything you say can and will be used against you in a court of law. You have the right to talk to a lawyer and have him present with you while you are being questioned. If you cannot afford to hire a lawyer, one will be appointed to represent you before any questioning, if you wish one."

Nearly anyone who has ever watched a police drama on television has heard this speech. In real life, thousands of police officers every day say the same words to criminal suspects before questioning them. This familiar police procedure has its roots in a legal decision made four decades ago. The case was called *Miranda v.* [versus] *Arizona*.

In 1963, Ernesto Miranda was convicted based on his signed confession. His lawyer appealed, arguing that Miranda did not know his rights. Three years later, the United States Supreme Court ruled that prosecutors may not use statements made by defendants unless the police have advised them of their rights. Miranda rights are now read to suspects upon their arrest, as in the above photo of a 1992 arrest in Los Angeles.

The story of *Miranda v. Arizona* began in 1963 with the arrest of a young man named Ernesto Miranda. But within a few short years, the case against Miranda had an important effect on far more than the fate of just one person. It changed the way police officers around the country do their jobs. It established new rules for the treatment of criminal suspects. And it brought national attention to a central issue in American law enforcement: How can the legal system balance the rights of the accused with the rights of law-abiding citizens?

A Rape in Arizona

In the early hours of March 3, 1963, a young woman was awakened by a loud pounding noise. Half asleep, she rushed to the door of her house. Standing outside was her eighteen-year-old sister, who was later known by the Arizona state court as Lois Ann Jameson.

Lois's sister, called Sarah by the court, barely recognized her. As Sarah later testified, Lois's hair was ruffled "like she had been in a fight," and her new suit "was a mess." Her sister asked her what was wrong, but Lois could not stop crying long enough to tell her. After about fifteen minutes, Lois calmed down and explained what had happened: She had just been raped.

THE CRIME

Several hours earlier, Lois had closed up the Paramount Theater in downtown Phoenix. As she did every Saturday, she had spent the night working there in the concession booth. She left the theater with a coworker, and the two caught a bus headed for the northeastern edge of the city. There, Lois lived with her sister, mother, and brother-in-law.

Just after midnight, Lois got off the bus alone. She started walking the few blocks from the bus stop to her house. Suddenly, a car backed out of a driveway, nearly hitting her as it pulled into the street. The car passed a couple of houses before coming to a stop. A man then got out and walked toward Lois. As he passed her, he grabbed her with one hand and put the other over her mouth. According to Lois's later court testimony, her attacker said, "If you don't scream, I won't hurt you."

The man yanked Lois back to his car and tied up her hands and ankles. He threw her into the backseat and told her to lie still. To make his point clear, the man shoved a sharp object into her neck, which she feared was a knife. He then got into the driver's seat and drove for twenty minutes until he reached the Arizona desert. Lois stayed quiet, too terrified to make a sound.

Lois's attacker stopped the car, got out, and opened the door to the backseat. He undressed Lois and raped her. He then asked her for money. She handed him all she had—four wrinkled $1 bills. Lois said nothing as they drove back into town. The rapist let her out a few blocks from her home. Lois later remembered that he said, "Whether you tell your mother what has happened or not is none of my business, but pray for me."

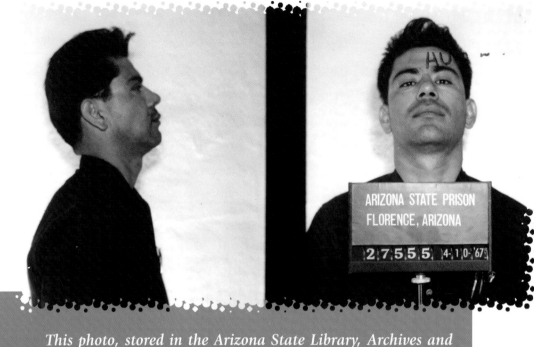

This photo, stored in the Arizona State Library, Archives and Public Records Division, was taken at the Phoenix police station on March 13, 1963, the morning that Ernesto Miranda was arrested. Miranda holds a placard with a number on it that helps identify him in police records. A complaint was then filed before Charles Coppock, justice of the peace, who set Miranda's bail at $3,000.

THE POLICE INVESTIGATE

Lois frantically told the whole story to Sarah. As soon as Lois was done, Sarah called the police. At 2:08 AM, an officer arrived at Lois's house. After speaking to her briefly, he took her to a nearby hospital. There, Lois recounted the rape to police detectives. She described her assailant: He was a Mexican man about twenty-seven or twenty-eight years old with a slight build. He was unshaven and was wearing glasses, jeans, and a T-shirt.

The next day, Lois went to the police station for a lineup. She looked carefully at the five men the police had rounded up, but none looked like her attacker. She also could not find her rapist in the police department's photographs of known sex offenders. The police began to wonder whether Lois was telling the truth. They were especially suspicious of her claim that she had tried to fight off the attacker, since there were no bruises on her body.

The police asked Lois to take a lie detector test. The test was inconclusive. It did not prove that she was telling the truth, but it did not prove that she was lying either. The police had no new leads, and they were not sure they could trust their witness. With the investigation at a standstill, they were ready to give up.

A BREAK IN THE CASE

After Lois was raped, she was too scared to walk alone from the bus stop after work. Her brother-in-law volunteered to meet her at the stop and escort her home each night. While waiting for her on Saturday, March 9—a week after the rape—Lois's brother-in-law spotted an old car parked down the road. It fit the description of the rapist's car that Lois had given the police. Though unsure about its model, she remembered it was painted light green and had worn brown upholstery inside. She also noted that a loop made of rope was attached to the back of the front seat. (The device was probably intended to give riders in the backseat something they could grab to help them get out of the car.)

The house at 2525 West Mariposa in Phoenix, Arizona, where Ernesto Miranda and Twila Hoffman lived at the time of Miranda's arrest. The green car with the rope loop sits in the driveway. Once meeting Miranda inside the house, Officers Cooley and Young immediately requested the young man accompany them to the police station. This 1963 photograph is now housed in the Arizona State Library, Archives and Public Records.

After Lois got off the bus that Saturday, she and her brother-in-law approached the parked car. As they got closer, the car started up and sped away. Still, her brother-in-law managed to copy down most of the license plate number. When Lois confirmed that it looked like her rapist's car, he called Officer Carroll Cooley, the detective in charge of Lois's case, with this new information.

Cooley discovered that the car belonged to a woman named Twila N. Hoffman. With Detective Wilfred Young, he went to her house, but no one was home. Her neighbors said she had moved out a few days earlier. Her live-in boyfriend, Ernesto Miranda, had left with her. He was a twenty-three-year-old Mexican American man with a mustache. Physically, he roughly fit Lois's description of her attacker.

Cooley and Young checked into Miranda's background. They found he had a troubled past. Since Miranda was fourteen, he had been in trouble with the law. He had spent years in and out of reform schools and prisons. Miranda had been convicted of several serious crimes, including robbery and assault with intent to commit rape.

Through post office records, the detectives found a new address for Miranda and Hoffman. On the morning of Wednesday, March 13, they arrived at the couple's house. In the driveway was an old green car. Inside, a rope loop hung from the back of the front seat. Cooley and Young were now sure they had found the man they were looking for.

Confessing to the Crime

Cooley and Young knocked on the door of Ernesto Miranda's house. His girlfriend, Twila Hoffman, answered. When the detectives asked to speak with Miranda, Hoffman went inside to wake him up. About an hour before, he had come home and gone to bed after working a twelve-hour shift at a Phoenix warehouse.

Still groggy, Miranda agreed to accompany the officers to the police station. "I didn't know whether I had a choice," he later explained to the *Arizona Daily Star*. Once in their car, he asked what was going on, but the detectives said they could not tell him. For the rest of the trip, Miranda sat nervously wondering what would come of his latest brush with the law.

THE INTERROGATION

At the station house, Miranda was placed in a lineup next to three other young Mexican American men recruited from the city jail. They all looked similar to Miranda. However, he was the only one wearing glasses and a T-shirt—items Lois Ann Jameson said her rapist had been wearing. Once the lineup was ready, the police called in Jameson. She carefully looked at the four men, but she could not say for sure that any of them was her rapist. Yet, she did say that Miranda's features and build

A photo of Miranda's arresting officer, Carroll F. Cooley, taken by the Phoenix Police Department on October 9, 1963. At the main police building, Cooley seated Miranda in interrogation room #2 and began his interview at approximately 10:30 AM. Cooley did not tell Miranda he had the right to remain silent.

most resembled those of her attacker.

After the lineup, Cooley and Young escorted Miranda to interrogation room #2. He asked, "How did I do?" One of the officers replied, "You flunked," even though Jameson had not been able to make a positive identification. The officer's comment, however, convinced Miranda that Jameson had fingered him as her rapist.

In the interrogation room, there was no tape or video recorder. There was also no attorney to advise Miranda. If there

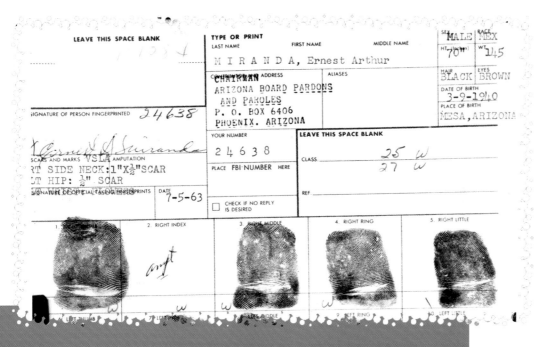

This is a picture of Ernesto Miranda's fingerprint chart, recorded by the Phoenix Police Division. In addition to all of his fingerprints, the chart lists basic information such as his name, date of birth, height, and weight. It also states specific physical characteristics of the individual. Note that under Ernesto Miranda's signature in the top left corner, there is mention of a scar on the right side of his neck. This record is housed at the Archives and Public Records department of the Arizona State Library.

had been, he or she would undoubtedly have told Miranda to keep quiet, since anything he said could be used against him in court. The detectives knew that Miranda had the right to remain silent, but they were not required by law to tell him so. Hoping for a confession, they were content to let Miranda think he had to answer their questions.

According to Cooley and Young, they spent the next two hours just talking to Miranda. During that time, the detectives said, they did not hurt Miranda, threaten him with violence, or promise to help clear him of any charges. Miranda, though, remembered the interrogation differently. According to Liva Baker's *Miranda: Crime, Law, and Politics,* he later recalled that the officers had tried to frighten him: "Once they get you in a little room and they start badgering you one way or the other, 'you better tell us . . . or we're going to throw the book at you' . . . that is what they told to me. They would throw the book at me." According to Miranda, they also suggested his criminal past was due to a mental problem and offered to get him medical help if he cooperated with them.

THE CONFESSION

Feeling pressured by the detectives, Miranda quickly broke down. He confessed he had raped Lois Ann Jameson. Cooley and Young continued their questioning. They asked Miranda if he was guilty of other local crimes. As Miranda recalled, "They mention first one crime, then another one, they are certain I am the person . . . knowing what a penitentiary is like, a person has to be frightened, scared."

Soon, Miranda confessed to two other crimes. He said he had robbed an eighteen-year-old woman of $8 in a parking lot the previous November. He also admitted he had tried to rape another woman a month before his attack on Jameson. Miranda later claimed the officers agreed to drop the rape charge if he confessed to the robbery. Cooley and Young, however, said they never made any such deal.

The detectives asked Miranda to write down his confession to the Jameson rape. They handed him a sheet of paper. At the top was a typed statement, which one of the officers read out loud. It said that, by signing the paper, Miranda was agreeing

Miranda v. Arizona

SUBJECT: Rape   D.R. 63-08380

STATEMENT OF: ERNEST ARTHER MIRANDA

TAKEN BY: C Cooley #413 - W. Young #182

DATE: 3-13-63   TIME: 1 30 Pm   PLACE TAKEN: Interr Rm #2

I, Ernest A. Miranda, do hereby swear that I make this statement voluntarily and of my own free will, with no threats, coercion, or promises of immunity, and with full knowledge of my legal rights, understanding any statement I make may be used against me.

I, Ernest A. Miranda, am 23 years of age and have completed the 8th grade in school.

Seen a girl walking up street stopped a little ahead of her got out of car, walked towards her grabbed her by the arm and asked to get in the car. Got in car without force tied hands + ankles. Drove away for a few miles. Stopped asked to take clothes off. Did not, asked me to take her back home. I started to take clothes off her without any force, and with cooperation. Asked her to lay down and she did. Could not get penis into vagina got about 1/2 (half) inch in. Told her to get clothes back on. Drove her home. I couldn't say I was sorry for what I had done. But asked her to say a prayer for me. EAM.

I have read and understand the foregoing statement and hereby swear to its truthfulness.

WITNESS: Carroll Cooley
Wilfred M. Young #182

This is a copy of Ernesto Miranda's written confession, composed on March 13, 1963, at a Phoenix, Arizona, police station. It also states the time, 1:30 PM, and the place, interrogation room #2, where the confession was written. The words at the top of the page list that the "subject" was rape and the confession was taken by Officers Cooley and Young. It is signed by Miranda at the bottom and witnessed by the police officers.

that he had confessed voluntarily and that he understood his rights under the law. It did not, however, explain what his rights were. In clumsy cursive, Miranda wrote out a description of the rape that sounded much like Jameson's account of the crime. At the bottom, he signed his name.

PREPARING A DEFENSE

That afternoon, Miranda was taken to jail. Two days later, he was brought before a justice of the peace for arraignment. The justice formally charged Miranda with rape and robbery. Following Arizona law, the justice also assigned a lawyer to represent Miranda at his trial, since Miranda did not have enough money to hire a lawyer himself.

Court-appointed attorneys were poorly paid. Most were young, inexperienced lawyers who were desperate for any kind of work. Miranda, however, was lucky. He was assigned Alvin Moore, a seventy-three-year-old attorney with forty years' experience practicing law in Arizona and Oklahoma. Moore did not enjoy trying criminal cases, but he felt it was his civic duty to help the poor defend themselves in court.

Moore quickly saw that Miranda did not have much of a case. With his written confession, it would be nearly impossible to convince a jury that he was not guilty. Out of desperation, Moore prepared to argue that Miranda was legally insane when he raped Jameson. Two court psychiatrists examined Miranda. Both agreed that Miranda had some mental problems. But they also agreed he knew the difference between right and wrong. As a result, Moore would not be able to use the insanity defense.

ON TRIAL

On June 19, 1963, Miranda went on trial for robbery. Within only a few hours, he was convicted. The following day, he was back in the courtroom, facing the charge that he raped Lois Ann Jameson.

Attorneys for the state of Arizona (the prosecution) called four people to testify against Miranda—Lois Ann Jameson, Sarah Jameson, and detectives Cooley and Young. The only dramatic moment in the trial was when Lois Ann Jameson took the stand. When describing the rape, she answered questions so quietly that the lawyers had to ask her to speak up. At one point on the stand, she began to cry. The jury found Jameson's testimony affecting. But the most compelling part of the prosecution's case was Miranda's written confession. It was the only document the prosecution entered into evidence.

In defending Miranda, Moore called no witnesses to the stand. He concentrated instead on his cross-examination of Jameson. With his questioning of Jameson, he drew the jury's attention to the inconsistencies in the story she had told to the police. He also brought up the fact that she had had no bruises on her body after the rape. In doing so, he tried to make the jury think that, since Jameson had not physically resisted the attack, she had not actually been raped.

Moore also asked the judge to throw out Miranda's confession. In cross-examining Cooley, the lawyer asked, "It is not your practice to advise people you arrest that they are entitled to the services of an attorney before they make a statement?" Cooley replied, "No, sir." On the basis of Cooley's answer, Moore requested that the judge suppress the confession because "the Supreme Court of the United States says a man is entitled to

Sentencing In Assault Case Set

6-21-636

Sentencing for Ernest Arthur Miranda, 23, of 2525 W. Mariposa, found guilty by a superior court jury of kidnaping and raping an 18-year-old girl, has been set for Thursday at 1:30 p.m. before Judge Yale McFate.

MIRANDA WAS prosecuted and convicted in a one-day trial. The nine men and three women who made up the jury deliberated a little over five hours before reaching the verdict.

The victim testified that Miranda pushed her into his car late at night as she was walking home from a bus stop, then took her out into the desert and raped her.

SHE SAID he threatened her with a sharp instrument when he first got her into the car, then tied her hands and feet with rope. After the assault, she said, he took her back to the general area of her home and let her out after asking her to pray for him.

In another trial Wednesday, Miranda was convicted of the $8 robbery last November of a 23-year-old women.

The June 21, 1963, edition of the Phoenix Gazette *reported the sentencing of Ernesto Miranda. The second paragraph of the article states that "Miranda was prosecuted and convicted in a one-day trial." Judge Yale McFate heard the case. The judge was also known for his involvement in the famous peyote dispute among states and Native Americans: In 1960, McFate overturned Arizona state law and allowed the use of the narcotic by Native Americans.*

an attorney at the time of his arrest." In fact, the United States Supreme Court—the highest court in the country—had never said this. Accordingly, the judge ignored Moore's request and allowed the jury to consider Miranda's confession in determining his guilt.

The jury discussed the case for five hours before arriving at a verdict. They found Miranda guilty of kidnapping and raping Jameson. On June 27, 1963, he was sentenced to serve twenty to thirty years in state prison. For his crimes against Jameson, it looked like Miranda would spend much of his life behind bars.

The Rights of the Accused

Alvin Moore had failed to convince the jury that Miranda was innocent. But Moore believed there was still a way he could help his client. He decided to appeal Miranda's case to the Arizona Supreme Court. This court was then the highest court in the state. It had the authority to throw out a decision made in a lower court, such as the one that convicted Miranda.

In December 1963, Moore submitted a brief—a short written statement—to the Arizona Supreme Court. In it, he argued that Miranda had not been given a fair trial. He claimed the lower court had made six legal errors when trying his client.

Five judges, called justices, served on the Arizona Supreme Court. They quickly decided that five of Moore's errors were not errors at all. But one possible error cited by Moore troubled them. It concerned Miranda's written confession. Moore argued in his brief that his client should have had a lawyer to advise him of his right to remain silent. If he had known about this right, Moore said, he never would have confessed. By Moore's reasoning, the confession was obtained illegally and, accordingly, should not have been presented to the jury.

GIDEON V. WAINWRIGHT

In making his argument, Moore referred to a decision in another recent case, *Gideon v. Wainwright* (1963). The defendant, Clarence Earl

After researching the law and the Constitution, Clarence Earl Gideon, shown here in 1961, realized that the Sixth Amendment had not been obeyed when the court refused to hire him a lawyer upon his arrest.

Gideon, was originally tried in Florida in 1961 for burglarizing a pool hall. Gideon said he was innocent and asked the court to appoint an attorney to represent him at his trial. (Gideon was too poor to hire a lawyer himself.) At the time, however, states were required to provide lawyers only for defendants who could be sentenced to death. Since Gideon was facing just a prison term, the judge refused his request. Gideon was found guilty and sentenced to five years in prison.

Two years later, Gideon's case was appealed to the United States Supreme Court. Its ruling was announced just a few days after Ernesto Miranda was arrested. All of the Court's nine justices found that Gideon had been unfairly denied a lawyer and ordered that he receive a new trial. Because of their decision, state courts would thereafter have to assign lawyers to represent at trial all poor defendants charged with serious crimes.

Moore saw similarities between Gideon's case and his client's. Both were convicted, in part, because they did not have the advice of a lawyer. There was one important difference in the two cases, however. Gideon never met with a lawyer, not even at his trial. Miranda did have Moore's help at the trial stage, though he was on his own during the interrogation. In his brief, Moore argued that it was just as important for a defendant to have legal help during questioning. By this reasoning, Miranda, like Gideon, had not been given a fair trial.

APPROACHING THE SUPREME COURT

After Moore presented the Arizona Supreme Court with his brief, the lawyers representing Arizona submitted one of their own. They laid out in writing their case, claiming that Moore's analysis was wrong. The justices read and discussed the two briefs. It took them a year and a half to issue their decision. In the end, they were not convinced by Moore's argument. The justices noted that Miranda, unlike Gideon, had never asked for a lawyer. They also thought it was important that Miranda had confessed of his own free will. According to Arizona law at the time, any voluntary confession could be presented to a jury as evidence.

The Rights of the Accused

Moore had lost his appeal. Feeling he had done his best, he gave up fighting for his client. Miranda, however, still had hope. He decided to appeal his case to the highest court in the land—the United States Supreme Court. Without a lawyer, he wrote to the Supreme Court, requesting a new trial.

While Miranda was waiting for a response, his case caught the attention of a lawyer named Robert Corcoran. Corcoran was the head of the Phoenix office of the American Civil Liberties Union (ACLU). Founded in 1920, the ACLU is an organ-

Taken in 1970, this photo of Justice Lorna Lockwood is housed at the Arizona State Library. Lockwood was chief justice of the Arizona Supreme Court when it ruled on the Miranda case. She was the first woman to serve as chief justice of a state supreme court and is considered to have had one of the biggest legal impacts of the 1960s.

ization devoted to protecting Americans' civil rights, including the rights of people accused of crimes.

Corcoran believed the Supreme Court might be interested in reviewing Miranda's case. But bringing a case to the Court was not easy. The Court picks and chooses which cases it wants to hear. The Court has only enough time to review about one out of every twenty cases presented.

THE SUPREME COURT OF THE UNITED STATES

The job of the Supreme Court of the United States is to review legal cases that were already tried in the state or federal court systems. It may choose to affirm (accept) or reverse (reject) a verdict handed down by a lower court. As the highest court in the country, the Supreme Court's decision in a case is final.

To ask the Supreme Court to take a second look at a case, a lawyer must submit a written document (a brief) in which he or she explains why the original decision was wrong. The lawyer must also argue why the case is important enough to merit the Supreme Court's attention.

Most of the cases that reach the Supreme Court deal with issues surrounding the U.S. Constitution. Often lower courts interpret a phrase in the Constitution in different ways. To settle such a dispute, the Supreme Court will choose a case that involves the issues in question. In its decision, the Supreme Court will declare its interpretation of the disputed phrase. Thereafter, all lower courts must follow this interpretation when making decisions on cases that hinge on similar constitutional issues.

ESCOBEDO V. ILLINOIS

Still, Corcoran had good reason to believe the Court would want to reexamine *Miranda v. Arizona*. Throughout the early 1960s, it had chosen to hear several cases that dealt with the rights of the accused. *Gideon v. Wainwright* was one such case.

The Rights of the Accused

Another was *Escobedo v. Illinois* (1964). In 1960, a twenty-two-year-old man named Danny Escobedo was arrested for the murder of his brother-in-law. While the police were interrogating him, Escobedo asked to see his lawyer. The police told Escobedo his lawyer did not want to help him. It was a lie. In fact, Escobedo's lawyer had heard about the arrest and had come to the station to advise his client. Hoping to get a confession from Escobedo, the police refused to let the lawyer into the interrogation room. Escobedo con-

Danny Escobedo's landmark case paved the way for Miranda v. Arizona. *Two years after the Supreme Court overturned his conviction in 1964, he was brought into a Chicago police station, as shown in this photograph taken in 1966, and charged with burglarizing a hot dog stand.*

fessed and was given a prison sentence of twenty years.

Four years after the crime, the Supreme Court reversed the conviction. It decided that Escobedo was entitled to a new trial because the police had been wrong to deny him the chance to consult his lawyer. *Escobedo v. Illinois* covered much of the same ground as *Gideon v. Wainwright*. But the cases were different in one important way. In reviewing *Gideon*, the Court had decided that a defendant had a right to an attorney at his or her trial. In its examination of *Escobedo*, the Court went even further. It found that a defendant had a right to a lawyer far earlier, during the interrogation stage.

NEW HOPE FOR MIRANDA

The finding was good news for Miranda. Like Escobedo, he did not have the advice of a lawyer during questioning. Since the Supreme Court felt Escobedo deserved a new trial, it might think Miranda did as well.

Corcoran recognized that the cases were not completely similar, however. Unlike Escobedo, Miranda had not asked to see a lawyer. He also could not afford to pay for one himself. Miranda's experience in the interrogation room, therefore, had differed from Escobedo's in two important ways—Miranda did not know his rights, and he had little money. But it was just these differences that made Corcoran think the Supreme Court would want to review Miranda's case. They suggested an important question of fairness: Was it right that Escobedo got a new trial and Miranda did not, just because Miranda had less money and knew less about the legal system?

Corcoran brought Miranda's case to the attention of the Phoenix law firm Lewis, Roca, Scoville, Beauchamps, and Linton. He convinced two of the firm's lawyers—John J. Flynn and John P. Frank—to try to take the case to the Supreme Court. Flynn was a skilled criminal trial lawyer, while Frank had a great deal of experience with appellate courts. They both agreed to work pro bono, or free of charge. In July 1965, they wrote to the Supreme Court, requesting that it hear Miranda's case. The following November, the Court responded. It agreed to review four cases involving confessions made during police interrogations. Among them was *Miranda v. Arizona*.

Making a Case

4

Flynn and Frank were thrilled to hear that the Supreme Court was willing to review *Miranda*. Arguing a case before the Court is a great honor for a lawyer. It was the first time either of Miranda's new attorneys had been invited to appear before the Court.

Just as excited by the news was Ernesto Miranda. Over the past three years, he had settled into life in prison. While there, he had been trained as a barber. He now spent much of his time cutting other inmates' hair. Miranda was still adjusting to the idea that he would remain in prison for many years when he got word that the Supreme Court would hear his case. He immediately sent a letter to Flynn and Frank, thanking them for their help.

WRITING THE BRIEF

For months before their Court appearance, Flynn and Frank worked hard to prepare. They first had to write a brief outlining the reasons why Miranda should be given a new trial. The lawyers did not try to argue that Miranda was not guilty. They said only that he was entitled to a new trial since he had been treated unfairly the first time he was tried.

Flynn and Frank bolstered their argument by citing portions of the U.S. Constitution. The Constitution was written in 1787, a few years after the United States became an independent nation. The document set out rules for how the U.S. government would be run.

In 1791, Congress added ten amendments (changes) to the document. Called the Bill of Rights, these amendments established that all Americans had certain rights and liberties, such as freedom of speech and freedom to practice whatever religion they choose. Over time, Congress added other amendments to the Constitution. The total number now stands at twenty-seven.

TWO AMENDMENTS

In constructing their case, Miranda's lawyers focused on two amendments—the Sixth and the Fourteenth. The Sixth Amendment deals with the rights of people accused of committing crimes. It states that the accused has a right to a speedy and public trial and a right to be told what crime he or she is charged with. But the part of the Sixth Amendment that most concerned Flynn and Frank was the accused's right "to have

Above is a copy of the United States Constitution's Fourteenth Amendment. This amendment was ratified, or made into law, in 1868. Originally, it was created to prevent state governments from taking rights away from former slaves after the Civil War (1861–1865). Now it is used to extend all individual freedoms granted in the Bill of Rights. Eventually, its interpretation became the core of the civil rights movement in the 1960s.

the assistance of counsel for his defense." Miranda did not have the advice of a lawyer when he wrote out his confession. His lawyers, therefore, claimed that presenting the confession to the jury was unconstitutional—that is, it violated a basic right guaranteed by the U.S. Constitution.

The Fourteenth Amendment was equally important to their case. This amendment was added to the Constitution in 1868, three years after the end of the Civil War (1861–1865). Its main purpose was to make former slaves citizens of the United States and of the states in which they lived. But it also forbade states from denying constitutional rights to any citizen. According to the Fourteenth Amendment, no state could "deprive any person of life, liberty, or property, without due process of law."

Originally, the Sixth Amendment, along with the other amendments in the Bill of Rights, was applied only to defendants in federal courts. But, Flynn and Frank argued, the Fourteenth Amendment extended the Bill of Rights to state courts as well. They said that Arizona, by denying Miranda's Sixth Amendment right to counsel, had deprived him of the "due process of law." (Courts have interpreted the phrase "due process of law" in slightly different ways. But essentially it refers to established legal procedures designed to protect the rights of the accused.) The Supreme Court was already familiar with this interpretation of the Fourteenth Amendment. It had played a role in several earlier Court decisions, including *Gideon* and *Escobedo*.

Both of these cases were also discussed in Flynn and Frank's brief. *Gideon* had established that the court had to assign a lawyer to a poor defendant tried for a serious crime. *Escobedo* had established that a suspect could have a lawyer advise him or her during an interrogation. With its ruling in *Miranda*, Flynn and Frank asked the Court to connect the dots between these two cases and *Miranda*. Like Gideon, they claimed, Miranda was entitled to a court-appointed lawyer. And like Escobedo, he was entitled to talk to one during questioning.

This photograph of Attorney General Gary K. Nelson of Arizona was taken in 1960 and resides in the Arizona State Library. The attorney general serves as chief legal officer of the state. The attorney general's office represents and provides legal advice to most state agencies.

OTHER OPINIONS

Several other briefs relating to the cases were submitted to the Supreme Court. One was written by Gary Nelson, the lawyer representing the state of Arizona. He argued that the state's trial against Miranda had been fair. He reminded the Court that the police had never threatened or physically hurt Miranda to get his confession. They also had never denied Miranda's request for an attorney, like the police who interrogated Escobedo had.

Nelson also made a strong argument against the idea that all defendants should be told about their right to counsel. He insisted that if lawyers were allowed in interrogation rooms, suspects would never confess. The practice would make an officer's job so difficult that many criminals would go free.

Along with *Miranda,* the Supreme Court was set to hear from lawyers involved in the three other confession cases. All of these lawyers also submitted briefs. The most interesting to the Court was the one written by Victor Earle from New York. He represented Michael Vignera, a defendant convicted of robbery. Earle's argument was similar to Flynn and Frank's, but he went a few steps further. Agreeing with Miranda's lawyers, he wrote that the police were "obliged to warn the accused of his absolute constitutional right to silence and of his right to consult with counsel *before* talking any further with police." But Earle went so far as suggesting how this warning should be worded: "[Y]ou have been placed under arrest. You are not required to say anything to us anytime or to answer any questions. Anything you say may be used as evidence in court. You may call a lawyer or a relative or a friend. Your lawyer may be present here, and you may talk with him. If you cannot obtain a lawyer, one will be appointed for you when your case first goes to court."

THE AMICUS BRIEFS

The Court was given three other briefs. Called amicus curiae ("friend of the court") briefs, these were submitted by organizations not directly involved in the cases. One organization represented twenty-nine state attorneys general. (An attorney general is the chief legal officer in a state or a country.) Another organization was made up of prosecuting attorneys. Both of these briefs cautioned the Court against making a ruling that would in any way interfere with police interrogations.

The third brief was submitted by the ACLU. It made many of the same points that Flynn and Frank did. But it argued that Miranda's confession was illegal not because of the Sixth Amendment, but because of the Fifth Amendment. This amendment deals with how criminal suspects should be tried. It includes the provision that a defendant "shall [not] be compelled in any criminal case to be a witness against himself." In other words, the courts are not allowed to force a suspect to say anything that might hurt his or her case.

The ACLU did not claim that the Phoenix police physically forced Miranda to confess. But they believed Miranda was so frightened in the interrogation room that he felt he had no choice. The ACLU said that police often violated the Fifth Amendment in their treatment of poor, uneducated suspects like Miranda. The interrogation room, it claimed, was a terrifying place to such defendants. Stuck in a hostile environment, unable to leave, battered by questions from several detectives, many defendants broke down and said too much. The ACLU concluded that the only way to guarantee their right to remain silent was to provide them with a lawyer. As the ACLU wrote, "[T]here is a need to provide the presence of someone at interrogation in whom the subject can confide and who will bolster his confidence."

When all were submitted, the nine justices began to sift through the various briefs. They then began the next phase of the four confession cases. The Court summoned Flynn, Frank, and all of the other lawyers involved to come to Washington, D.C., on February 18, 1966, to present oral arguments. On that day, *Miranda v. Arizona* would finally be reviewed by the Supreme Court.

THE OTHER CASES

Along with *Miranda v. Arizona*, the Supreme Court heard three other cases dealing with issues surrounding confessions obtained during police interrogations.

- *Vignera v. New York*: Michael Vignera was arrested for robbing a shop in Brooklyn, New York. The police interrogated Vignera for eight hours but never told him he had a right to remain silent. The interrogation finally ended when Vignera signed a confession. He was convicted and lost his later appeal.

- *California v. Stewart:* In Los Angeles, California, the police arrested Roy Stewart for murder and robbery. They interrogated him nine times over five days, and he confessed. Stewart was convicted, but the California Supreme Court overturned the ruling because of the interrogation tactics.

- *Westover v. United States:* Carl Westover was arrested in Kansas City, Missouri, for robbery. The next day, the FBI took custody of Westover, who was wanted for two bank robberies in California. During questioning by the FBI, he signed a written confession that included a printed paragraph saying he understood his rights. Westover was tried in federal court and was convicted.

The Supreme Court Decision

5

On the court date, Flynn and Frank entered the Supreme Court Building. They walked down the Great Hall, lined with busts of former Supreme Court justices, to the courtroom. With seating for three hundred, this enormous oak-paneled room was filled with marble sculptures representing law and justice. At the front was a huge red velour curtain. When each session of the Court began, the nine justices, all dressed in black robes, emerged from behind the curtain to take their seats on the elevated bench along the room's east wall.

The two attorneys had spent many long months preparing for this day. Now the case—and Ernesto Miranda's fate—would rest on their presentation to the Court. Miranda's legal team would have only thirty minutes to convince the justices that he deserved a new trial. During the oral arguments, the justices were permitted

Miranda v. Arizona

The nine distinguished justices who made up the Supreme Court in 1966 when Miranda v. Arizona was presented. They are, from left to right: Justice William Brennan, Justice Potter Stewart, Justice Byron White, Justice Hugo Black, Justice Abe Fortas, Justice William O. Douglas, Justice John Marshall Harlan, Chief Justice Earl Warren, and Justice Tom C. Clark. This photograph was taken in 1965 in the east conference room in the Supreme Court Building.

to interrupt with questions. As part of their preparations, Flynn and Frank had come up with a good answer for any question the justices might ask.

Both of Miranda's lawyers sat in the area assigned to defense attorneys. However, only Flynn would speak before the Court. With fifteen years as a criminal lawyer, he had much more hands-on experience in police stations than Frank. As quoted in Liva Baker's *Miranda: Crime, Law, and Politics*, Frank explained that this was the reason he thought Flynn should explain their case to the justices: "What the Court really wants to hear more than anything are the practical aspects of what happens down in the police interrogation room from the fellow who is there handling it on a day-to-day basis."

ARGUING BEFORE THE COURT

Out of the four confession cases to be heard, the Court had chosen *Miranda* as the lead case. Flynn was, therefore, the first lawyer to speak that day. Although he later claimed he was "scared to death," he made a forceful presentation. He told the justices about Miranda's poverty, mental problems, and lack of education. Flynn wanted to make it clear to the justices that Miranda had not asked for a lawyer because he had been unaware of his Sixth Amendment right to counsel.

The justices, though, seemed more interested in another defense theory—the ACLU's idea that Miranda's Fifth Amendment right to remain silent had been violated. Justice Byron R. White particularly pressed Flynn to discuss whether Miranda had felt compelled to confess. Flynn argued that he

Miranda v. Arizona

This photograph of Chief Justice Earl Warren was taken on March 19, 1966. In addition to ruling on Miranda v. Arizona, Warren also headed the commission that investigated the assassination of President John F. Kennedy in 1963. Warren died in Washington, D.C., in 1974.

had: "[T]he denial of the right to counsel at the stage in the proceeding when he most certainly needed it . . . could, in and of itself . . . constitute compulsion." Justice Hugo Black appeared to accept Flynn's argument. He said the accused did not need to have "a gun pointed at his head" to feel an overwhelming pressure to confess. Black suggested that "[police] control and custody" could be a "kind of compulsion," leading some defendants to say too much.

Flynn's half hour before the Court was soon up. But the discussion of Miranda and the other confession cases continued. Each lawyer who had submitted a brief had a chance to speak. In all, the Court heard eight hours of oral arguments over three days. On Wednesday, March 2, 1966, the arguments were finally completed. Earl Warren—the chief justice, or head, of the Supreme Court—thanked the lawyers, particularly expressing his appreciation to those who had worked for free. Miranda v. Arizona and the other confession cases were now in the hands of the Supreme Court justices. They would be the final word on whether Miranda would be granted a new trial.

THE COURT RULES

More than three months passed before the Supreme Court was ready to announce its decision. During that time, the justices privately debated the issues brought up by *Miranda* and voted on whether he and the other defendants were entitled to new trials. Not all of the justices had to agree on the decision. The final ruling needed to be approved only by a majority of the nine judges.

Much of the public was anxiously awaiting word from the Supreme Court. Lawyers and police officers were certainly interested in the *Miranda* decision, since its outcome could have a big impact on how they did their jobs. But many people outside of law enforcement were also curious about the case. In the early 1960s, crime was on the rise. As a result, law and order were becoming hot political issues. Some politicians were speaking out against recent Supreme Court decisions that helped protect the rights of the accused, claiming that they made it hard for the police to fight crime. These politicians worried that this trend would continue with the Court's ruling on *Miranda*.

On Monday, June 13, 1966, the Supreme Court was ready to reveal its findings to the public. Not surprisingly, the courtroom was packed that day. Chief Justice Earl Warren chose to read the majority decision himself. Often, the Court presented only a summary of its ruling. But Warren felt the *Miranda* case was so important that he read the Court's entire sixty-page written decision. For more than an hour, the crowd sat silently as Warren's voice filled the courtroom.

Miranda v. Arizona

The Escobedo cases raise constitutional issues
Basically the issue is under the 5ᵗʰ Amend—
the prohibition against compelling a person to be a witness against himself
It might also raise the question of right to counsel
(6ᵗʰ) as in Escobedo where the lawyer was present and
was not permitted to see his client, but
where there is interrogation in the last analysis it always goes back to 5ᵗʰ

The fundamental question is not whether a
deft. can talk to the police without benefit of counsel after he is in
custody but whether he can be interrogated
Exclamatory or spontaneous or where a person suddenly out of the police confessions or remorseful
admissions etc. are not barred

Defts right to counsel unless he knowingly
and intelligently waves it commences at
least when he is taken into custody
(under some circumstances before arrest)

The police have no right to arrest a person
or take him into custody against his will for the purpose
of interrogation
And whatever reason they assign for depriving him of his liberty
his right to counsel commences at least

Pictured above is a page of notes written by Chief Justice Earl Warren, now housed in the Library of Congress. Warren begins with thoughts on the Escobedo case, (Escobedo v. Illinois). When judges write opinions, they must cite precedents. Judges must include the way they apply to a given situation and make references to regulations and prior decisions made in the courts. They may also use secondary literature such as journal articles.

THE DECISION

Within a few minutes, the majority's opinion became clear. Five of the justices—Hugo Black, William Douglas, William Brennan, Abe Fortas, and Earl Warren—agreed that Miranda and the other defendants deserved new trials. They believed that the defendants' confessions should not have been admitted into evidence because their Fifth Amendment right to remain silent had been violated. As Warren read, "[A]t the outset, if a person in custody is to be subjected to interrogation, he must first be informed in clear and unequivocal [unquestionable] terms that he has the right to remain silent."

Supreme Court Justice William J. Brennan Jr. in a photograph taken in 1972, in Washington, D.C. The son of struggling Irish immigrants, Brennan was appointed to the Court in 1956 by President Dwight D. Eisenhower. During Brennan's thirty-four-year term, he offered over 1,000 opinions on a range of subjects. He died in 1997.

According to the five justices, the police also needed to tell suspects that, if they spoke, anything they said could be used against them in court. In addition, the Court declared that having a lawyer in the interrogation room was "indispensable" to protecting a suspect's rights. The justices, therefore, required that the police explain to suspects that they had a right to a lawyer. If a suspect wanted a lawyer but could not afford one, the court was obligated to assign him one free of charge.

Supreme Court of the United States
Washington 25, D. C.

CHAMBERS OF
JUSTICE WM. J. BRENNAN, JR.

May 11, 1966

RE: Nos. 759, 760, 761 and 584.

Dear Chief:

I am writing out my suggestions addressed to your Miranda opinion with the thought that we might discuss them at your convenience. I feel guilty about the extent of the suggestions but this will be one of the most important opinions of our time and I know that you will want the fullest expression of my views.

I have one major suggestion. It goes to the basic thrust of the approach to be taken. In your very first sentence you state that the root problem is "the role society must assume, consistent with the federal Constitution, in prosecuting individuals for crime." I would suggest that the root issue is "the restraints society must observe, consistent with the federal Constitution, in prosecuting individuals for crime."

Shown above is a memo written by Justice William J. Brennan Jr. to Chief Justice Earl Warren on Supreme Court letterhead. Dated May 11, 1966, the memo is a response to Warren's draft of the majority opinion for Miranda v. Arizona. *Opinions can take a long time and a great deal of effort to complete. Brennan writes, "This will be one of the most important opinions of our time . . ." The memo is located in the Library of Congress in Washington, D.C.*

A *clipping from the* New York Times *from June 14, 1966, the day after the U.S. Supreme Court ruled on* Miranda v. Arizona. *The article contains excerpts from the judges' opinions, including sections of text by two dissenting (disagreeing) judges: Justice Byron R. White and Justice John Marshall Harlan. The article begins with the "Opinion of the Court," the majority opinion written by Chief Justice Warren.*

DISSENTING VIEWS

Four of the Supreme Court justices—Potter Stewart, Tom C. Clark, John M. Harlan, and Byron R. White—strongly disagreed with the majority decision. Clark, Harlan, and White wrote down their views in dissenting opinions. The minority justices believed that Miranda's constitutional rights had not been violated since he had willingly confessed. Unlike their colleagues, they felt that lawyers had no place in the interrogation room. Their presence, Harlan wrote, would "ultimately . . . discourage any confession at all." White had an even more serious prediction for what the decision would mean: "In some unknown number of cases the Court's rule will return a killer, a rapist or other criminal to the streets . . . to repeat his crime whenever it pleases him."

The *Miranda* decision was on the front page of newspapers all over the country. (Miranda himself learned about the decision from the evening television news.) Many people—especially police officers—were upset by the news, convinced that it would mean more criminals would go free. Others supported the decision. They argued that it would make the legal system more fair and help the poor find justice. Legal experts, law enforcement officials, and concerned citizens all weighed in with their opinions about the case, which stayed in the news for months. But few could know that the debate over *Miranda* was only beginning.

The Legacy of Miranda

6

$\mathbf{A}$s experts discussed the fine points of *Miranda*, police departments were busy with a more practical matter—adjusting to the changes the *Miranda* decision brought to the station house. The Supreme Court had not specified exactly what police were to say to suspects before interrogating them. Soon, however, most departments began instructing police officers to recite more or less the same words: "You have the right to remain silent. Anything you say can and will be used against you in a court of law. You have the right to talk to a lawyer and have him present with you while you are being questioned. If you cannot afford to hire a lawyer, one will be appointed to represent you before any questioning, if you wish one." The speech became known as the Miranda warning.

At first, police officers and detectives had trouble remembering the entire warning. To help them out, many

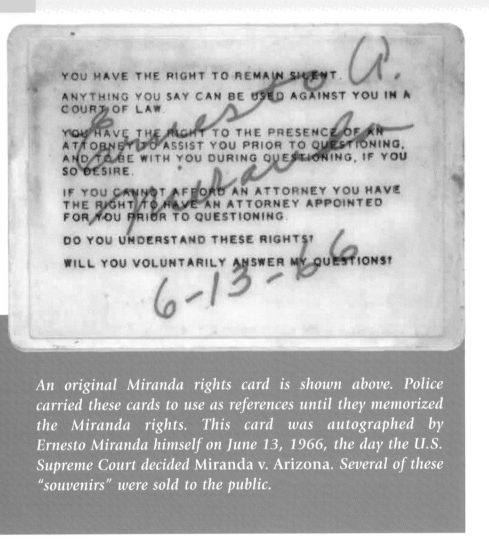

YOU HAVE THE RIGHT TO REMAIN SILENT.

ANYTHING YOU SAY CAN BE USED AGAINST YOU IN A COURT OF LAW.

YOU HAVE THE RIGHT TO THE PRESENCE OF AN ATTORNEY TO ASSIST YOU PRIOR TO QUESTIONING, AND TO BE WITH YOU DURING QUESTIONING, IF YOU SO DESIRE.

IF YOU CANNOT AFFORD AN ATTORNEY YOU HAVE THE RIGHT TO HAVE AN ATTORNEY APPOINTED FOR YOU PRIOR TO QUESTIONING.

DO YOU UNDERSTAND THESE RIGHTS?

WILL YOU VOLUNTARILY ANSWER MY QUESTIONS?

An original Miranda rights card is shown above. Police carried these cards to use as references until they memorized the Miranda rights. This card was autographed by Ernesto Miranda himself on June 13, 1966, the day the U.S. Supreme Court decided Miranda v. Arizona. *Several of these "souvenirs" were sold to the public.*

departments issued Miranda cards—pieces of paper printed with the warning that police officers could carry in their pockets. However, after reading the warning day after day, they eventually committed the words to memory. In a short time, both police officers and career criminals knew the Miranda warning by heart.

MIRANDA AND THE POLICE

Police officers around the country just as quickly learned the importance of reading the Miranda warning. According to the rules set out by the Supreme Court, if a suspect confessed during questioning, the confession could be used in court only if he or she had been read the Miranda rights. The police also had to adjust to several other new rules for the interrogation room. If, after being Mirandized, a suspect said he or she did not want to say anything, the police had to stop their questioning immediately. They also had to end the interrogation if the suspect said he or she wanted to talk with a lawyer.

Some police officials were slow to adopt these new procedures. They were used to conducting their interrogations their own way and resented being told what to say to suspects. Many were also convinced that, once they read the Miranda warning to a suspect, they would never get a confession.

Despite their concerns, police interrogators still had a fairly free reign over what they said to suspects. They could not beat or threaten people in their custody, but they were allowed to lie or trick them. Some police officers learned to read the Miranda warning in a quiet, bored voice, hoping the suspect would not pay attention. Others implied that if the suspect did not waive the right to see a lawyer, he or she would be in even worse trouble. Still others took their time finding a lawyer for a suspect after he or she asked for one. They thought that, if they stalled long enough, the suspect would crack and confess before the lawyer arrived.

In most cases, though, the interrogators found they did not have to resort to trickery. Even after hearing their Miranda warning, most suspects were willing to talk. Some probably did not understand their rights, but most answered the interrogators' questions either out of fear or out of the hope that the police would go easier on them if they did. Over the years, many studies have shown the same thing: the number of confessions have dropped only slightly since the Supreme Court's ruling. According to the *New Republic*, today the vast majority of suspects—between 80 and 90 percent—choose to waive their rights and talk to the police without the benefit of legal counsel.

COURT CHALLENGES

Despite these studies, *Miranda* has continually been attacked for keeping lawbreakers out of jail. Just two years after the Court's decision, Republican presidential candidate Richard Nixon placed *Miranda* at the forefront of his campaign. He said that the Supreme Court under Earl Warren was more concerned with protecting criminals than law-abiding citizens. If elected, Nixon promised to replace Warren, who was due to retire, with a more conservative chief justice.

Nixon won, and true to his word, he appointed Warren Burger as the chief justice of the Supreme Court. Burger had been very critical of the *Miranda* decision. His Court heard several cases that challenged the ruling. In a few of its decisions, the Court weakened the power of *Miranda* by allowing some statements made by un-Mirandized suspects to be admitted into evidence. For instance, in *Michigan v. Tucker* (1974), the police told the suspect that he had a right to remain silent but not that he had a right to a lawyer. The suspect then made a statement in which he identified a witness to the crime. Even though the suspect had not been read a complete Miranda warning, the Burger Court concluded that the evidence he provided in his statement could be used against him. Another important case relating to *Miranda* was *New York v. Quaries*. In this case, an armed suspected rapist was chased into a crowded supermarket by a police officer. The officer caught the suspect and, before Mirandizing him, asked where his gun was. The Supreme Court ruled that the gun could be entered into evidence even though the suspect made a statement about it before he was read his rights.

United States Supreme Court Associate Justice William Rehnquist poses in his chambers in Washington, D.C. Although he was nominated by President Richard Nixon as an associate justice in 1972, it was President Ronald Reagan who appointed Rehnquist chief justice in 1986.

In 1986, Judge William Rehnquist became the new chief justice of the Supreme Court. The Rehnquist Court has continued to hear cases challenging the *Miranda* decision, but it has yet to be reversed. The most recent challenge was *Dickerson v. United States* (2000). Citing a long-ignored law passed by Congress in 1968, a lawyer in the case claimed that confessions of suspects who have not been Mirandized should be admissible in court. If he had persuaded the Court, the police would no longer have to read Miranda warnings before interrogations. However, in a seven-to-two decision, the Supreme Court found that the *Miranda* decision of 1966 should still stand. On behalf of his Court, Chief Justice Rehnquist explained that *Miranda* has become such an accepted part of the American legal system that the justices saw

In this photograph, taken on February 15, 1967, in Phoenix, Arizona, Ernesto Miranda (right) speaks with his attorney, John J. Flynn (left) on the first day of his new trial. Even though the Supreme Court's ruling gave Miranda a second chance in court, he was again convicted.

no reason to overturn it: "We do not think there is such justification for overruling *Miranda*. *Miranda* has become embedded in routine police practice to the point where the warnings have become part of our national culture."

THE FATE OF ERNESTO MIRANDA

Ernesto Miranda's last name is now known to just about any American who has ever watched a crime show or passed through a station house. But his famous name did little to help the man himself.

As a result of the 1966 Supreme Court ruling in *Miranda v. Arizona*, Miranda was granted a new trial. John Flynn agreed to serve as Miranda's lawyer. At first, it looked as though Miranda would win his case. Because of the Supreme Court decision, the state of Arizona could not use his written confession against him at his second trial. The prosecution still had Lois Ann Jameson's testimony, but she was not a very reliable witness. As the trial began on February 15, 1967, many in the courtroom believed that, at its end, Miranda would be a free man.

But Miranda's hopes were quickly dashed by a surprise witness—his former girlfriend, Twila Hoffman. Miranda and Hoffman were involved in a custody battle over their young daughter, Cleopatra. Hoffman became so angry at Miranda that she went to the Phoenix police. She claimed that three days after he had originally confessed, he admitted to her that he had raped Lois Ann Jameson. Hoffman repeated her story at Miranda's trial. It was enough to convince the jury that he was guilty. Miranda was given the same sentence he received four years before—twenty to thirty years in prison.

While imprisoned, Miranda earned a high school diploma and took a few college classes. Because of his good behavior, he was paroled (released early) in 1974. Within months, however, he was back in prison. A policeman who stopped Miranda for driving recklessly found drugs and a gun in his car. Possession of both items was a violation of his parole.

F-661-63

closed

LAW OFFICES

FLYNN KIMERER THINNES & GALBRAITH

JOHN J. FLYNN
MICHAEL D. KIMERER
THOMAS A. THINNES
TOM GALBRAITH
RICHARD L. PARRISH
CLARK L. DERRICK

1950 FIRST NATIONAL BANK PLAZA
100 WEST WASHINGTON STREET
PHOENIX, ARIZONA 85003
TELEPHONE (602) 254-6511

6138 TRANSAMERICA TITLE BUILDING
177 NORTH CHURCH STREET
TUCSON, ARIZONA 85701
(602) 884-7530

September 21, 1973

Mrs. Twila Spears
209 West Juniper Circle
Mesa, Arizona

Dear Mrs. Spears:

    I am writing to you on behalf of Ernesto Miranda. He has indicated to me that he is desirous of having some visitation rights with his daughter, Cleopatra Miranda. He is not desirous of causing any difficulty with you or anyone else, nor is he in any way harboring any hard feelings toward anyone, including yourself. He simply would like the right to occasionally visit with his daughter. He indicated that he did not want to personally contact you or bother you in any way and therefore requested that I write to you concerning the problem.

    I would appreciate it if you would advise me concerning your position as to Ernesto having visitation with his daughter and under what circumstances they would be allowed.

    I remain,

Very truly yours,

John J. Flynn

JJF:vd

cc: Mr. Ernesto Miranda

October 1, 1973

Flynn, Kimerer, Thinnes & Galbraith
100 W. Washington St.
Phoenix, Arizona 85003

Dear Mr. Flynn;

In answer to the enclosed letter

NO

This letter is very close to harrassement

Any other correspondence as to this matter will result in Legal action

Yours truly,

Twila Mae Spears

CC to: Moise Berger
County Attorney

This letter is from Ernesto Miranda's lawyer, John J. Flynn, to Miranda's former girlfriend, Twila Spears (Hoffman). The letter is a request for visitations with the daughter they shared. Spears's response letter (inset) reads simply, "No." The letter from Flynn is dated September 21, 1973, and is from the law offices of Flynn, Kimerer, Thinnes, and Galbraith. Hoffman's response came a short time later, on October 1, 1973.

Miranda, Rights Ruling Subject, Killed In Fight

Ariz. Daily Star, Tucson

PHOENIX (AP) — Ernesto Miranda, whose name was on a landmark Supreme Court decision requiring police to inform defendants of their rights, was stabbed to death last night in a fight over a card game in a Skid Row bar, police said.

Miranda, 34, was dead on arrival at a Phoenix hospital after being stabbed once in the upper left chest and once in the abdomen. He was stabbed by one of two men he had beaten in a fistfight minutes earlier, said Patrolman Gordon Costa at the La Amapola bar. 2-1-1976

One of the men, described by witnesses as an illegal Mexican immigrant, was taken to police headquarters for questioning, officers said. The killer, also believed to be an illegal Mexican immigrant, fled and was being sought by police in the area of a downtown

there they started interrogating me about a kidnap case . . . .

"This went on for a couple of hours. In the process I was taken out of one interrogation room and into another."

The police questioned him about two robberies and put him in a lineup, after which they told him a victim had singled him out "so I might as well admit to the crime," Miranda had recalled.

He said that officers offered to make a deal — confess to the kidnaping and they would drop the robbery charges. "So I made the statement," Miranda said.

But when he got to court he was told he was still charged with robbery. Miranda said he repeatedly asked for a lawyer but was denied one.

This Arizona Daily Star newspaper article is housed at the Arizona Historical Society. It is dated February 1, 1976, the morning after Ernesto Miranda was stabbed to death in a bar in Phoenix, Arizona. He was thirty-four years old. The article discusses how the fight in the bar broke out and cites the U.S. Supreme Court case that bears Miranda's name.

In April 1975, Miranda was again freed. He found a string of low-paying jobs but added to his income by selling autographed Miranda cards for a couple dollars apiece. On the night of January 31, 1976, he took his sorrows to a Phoenix bar. There, he got into a fistfight with two men. One had a knife. He stabbed Miranda in the stomach and chest. Miranda died before he could reach the hospital. The killer escaped, but the police caught the other man. On the way to the police station, an officer read him his Miranda rights.

Glossary

appeal Review by a higher court of a law case previously decided in a lower court.

arraignment Legal proceeding during which an accused person is called before a court to answer a charge.

brief A document submitted to a court by a lawyer outlining a legal argument.

cross-examination Questioning of a witness in a court case by the lawyer of the opposing side.

due process Established legal procedures designed to protect the rights of the accused.

inadmissible Not allowed to be heard as evidence in a court of law.

interrogation Questioning a person, particularly by police or other law enforcement officials.

jury A group of people responsible for handing down a verdict in a legal trial.

justice A judge.

lineup A group of people, standing in a line, from which police ask a crime witness to identify the guilty party.

Mirandize To read Miranda warnings to a criminal suspect.

oral argument A legal argument spoken by a lawyer to a jury or judge.

prosecution   Legal team that presents the case against a person charged with a crime.

rape   The crime of forcing a person to perform a sexual act.

Supreme Court   The highest court of the United States, whose legal decisions affect all other courts in the country.

suspect   A person suspected of committing a crime.

unconstitutional   In violation of the principles set out in the U.S. Constitution.

verdict   The decision of a jury at the end of a trial.

For More Information

American Civil Liberties Union
125 Broad Street, 18th Floor
New York, NY 10004
(212) 344-3005
Web site: http://www.aclu.org

Supreme Court Historical Society
Opperman House
224 East Capitol Street NE
Washington, DC 20003
(202) 543-0400
Web site: http://www.supremecourthistory.org

United States Supreme Court
Public Information Officer
Supreme Court of the United States
Washington, DC 20543
(202) 479-3211
Web site: http://www.supremecourtus.gov

Web Sites

Due to the changing nature of Internet links, the Rosen Publishing Group, Inc., has developed an online list of Web sites related to the subject of this book. This site is updated regularly. Please use this link to access the list:

http://www.rosenlinks.com/scctps/miaz

For Further Reading

Cornelius, Kay. *The Supreme Court*. Philadelphia: Chelsea House Publishers, 2000.

Gold, Susan Dudley. *Miranda v. Arizona: Suspects' Rights*. New York: Twenty-First Century Books, 1995.

Owens, Lois Smith, and Vivian Verdell Gordon. *Think About Prisons and the Criminal Justice System*. New York: Walker, 1992.

Pascoe, Elaine. *America's Courts on Trial: Questioning Our Legal System*. Brookfield, CT: Millbrook Press, 1997.

Patrick, John J. *The Supreme Court of the United States: A Student Companion*. 2nd edition. New York: Oxford University Press, 2002.

Quiri, Patricia Ryon. *The Bill of Rights*. New York: Children's Press, 1998.

Quiri, Patricia Ryon. *The Constitution*. New York: Children's Press, 1998.

Wice, Paul B. *Gideon v. Wainwright and the Right to Counsel*. New York: Franklin Watts, 1995.

Wice, Paul B. *Miranda v. Arizona: "You Have the Right to Remain Silent . . ."* New York: Franklin Watts, 1996.

Wormser, Richard. *Defending the Accused: Stories from the Courtroom*. New York: Franklin Watts, 2001.

Bibliography

Baker, Liva. *Miranda: Crime, Law, and Politics.* New York: Atheneum, 1985.

"Criminal Law in the 1960s." Discovering U.S. History. Gale Research, 1997. Reproduced in History Resource Center. Farmington Hills, MI: Gale Group. Retrieved September 8, 2001 (http://galenet.galegroup.com/serviet/HistRC).

"Gideon v. Wainwright." Great American Court Cases. Four vols. Gale Group, 1999. Reproduced in History Resource Center. Farmington Hills, MI: Gale Group. Retrieved September 11, 2002 (http://galenet.galegroup.com/servellet/HistRC).

Hogrogian, John. *Miranda v. Arizona: The Rights of the Accused.* San Diego: Lucent Books, 1999.

Kamisar, Yale. *"Miranda v. Arizona." The Oxford Companion to the U.S. Supreme Court,* edited by Kermit Hall. New York: Oxford University Press, 1992.

"Miranda Rights." *NewsHour with Jim Lehrer* transcript. January 6, 2000. Retrieved September 1, 2002 (http://www.pbs.org/newshour/bb/law/jan-june00/miranda_1-6.html).

"Miranda v. Arizona." Great American Court Cases. Four vols. Gale Group, 1999. Reproduced in History Resource Center. Farmington Hills, MI: Gale Group. Retrieved June 12, 2002 (http://galenet.galegroup.com/serviet/HistRC).

Bibliography

"*Miranda v. Arizona* (1966)" Landmark Cases: Supreme Court. Retrieved September 16, 2002 (http://www.landmarkcases.org/miranda/beyond.html).

Richey, Warren. "Miranda Warning Survives." *Christian Science Monitor*, Vol. 92, No. 151, June 27, 2000, p. 1.

Rosen, Jeffrey. "Right Should Remain Silent." *New Republic*, Vol. 222, No. 18, May 1, 2000, p. 18.

Primary Source Image List

Cover: Photograph of Ernesto Miranda (left) in police lineup. Taken in 1963 in Phoenix, Arizona. Housed in the Arizona State Library, Archives and Public Records.

Page 5: Photograph of police officers carrying an arrested man. Taken in Los Angeles on April 30, 1992, by Peter Turnley.

Page 8: Mug shot photograph of Ernesto Miranda. Taken in 1963 by the Phoenix Police Department in Phoenix, Arizona. Housed in the Arizona State Library, Archives and Public Records.

Page 10: Photograph of Ernesto Miranda's home in Phoenix, Arizona. Taken in 1963 by the Phoenix Police Department. Housed in the Arizona State Library, Archives and Public Records.

Page 13: Photograph of Officer Carroll Cooley, taken on October 9, 1963, in Phoenix, Arizona, by the Phoenix Police Department.

Page 14: Ernesto Miranda's fingerprint chart. Recorded on July 5, 1963, by the Phoenix Police Department. Housed in the Arizona State Library, Archives and Public Records.

Page 16: Signed confession written by Ernesto Miranda on March 13, 1963, in the Phoenix Police Department.

Page 19: Newspaper clipping from the June 21, 1963, edition of the *Phoenix Gazette.* Filed in the *Phoenix Gazette* archives.

Page 21: Photograph of Clarence Earl Gideon. Taken in 1961.

Page 23: Photograph portrait of Lorna Lockwood. Taken in 1970 in Arizona.

Page 25: Photograph of Danny Escobedo. Taken in Chicago, Illinois, on November 3, 1966.

Page 29: Reproduction of the Fourteenth Amendment. Created in 1868.

Page 31: Photograph of Gary Nelson. Taken in 1960 in Phoenix, Arizona.

Page 36: Photograph portrait of the Supreme Court. Taken on November 10, 1965, in the East Conference Room of the U.S. Supreme Court Building.

Page 38: Photograph of Chief Justice Earl Warren. Taken in the U.S. Supreme Court Building on March 19, 1966.

Page 40: Notes written by Chief Justice Earl Warren. Created in 1966 in Washington, D.C. Housed in the Library of Congress.

Page 41: Photograph of William Brennan. Taken in Washington, D.C., in 1972.

Page 42: Memo to Chief Justice Earl Warren. Written by William Brennan on May 11, 1966. Housed in the Library of Congress.

Page 43: Newspaper clipping from the June 14, 1966, edition of the *New York Times*. Filed in the *New York Times* archives.

Page 46: Miranda card signed by Ernesto Miranda on June 13, 1966. Privately owned.

Page 49: Photograph of William Rehnquist. Taken on June 19, 1986, in Washington, D.C.

Page 50: Photograph of John Flynn and Ernesto Miranda. Taken in Phoenix, Arizona, on February 15, 1967.

Page 52: Letter to Twila Spears from John Flynn. Written on September 21, 1973, in Phoenix, Arizona. Letter from Twila Spears to John Flynn. Written on October 1, 1973.

Page 53: Newspaper clipping from the February 1, 1976, edition of the *Arizona Daily Star*. Filed in the *Arizona Daily Star* archives, Tuscon, Arizona.

Index

About the Author

Liz Sonneborn is a writer and an editor living in Brooklyn, New York. A graduate of Swarthmore College, she has written more than thirty books for children and adults, including *The American West*, *A to Z of American Women in the Performing Arts*, and *The New York Public Library's Amazing Native American History*, winner of a 2000 Parent's Choice Award.

Photo Credits

Eagle on back cover and throughout interior © Eyewire; Red curtain throughout interior © Arthur S. Aubry/PhotoDisc; Wood grain on cover and back cover and throughout interior © M. Angelo/Corbis; Cover #97-7381, p. 8 #00-0517, p. 10 #97-7384, pp. 14, 16, p. 23 #97-7013, p. 31 #97-7483, p. 52 Arizona State Library, Archives and Public Records, Archives Division, Phoenix; p. 5 © Peter Turnley/Corbis; p.13 Courtesy Carroll Cooley; p.19 © Phoenix Gazette, June 21, 1963, used with permission, permission does not imply endorsement; pp. 21, 25, 38, 49, 50 © Bettmann/Corbis; p. 29 General Records of the United States Government, National Archives and Records Administration; p. 36 Joseph J. Scherschel/ National Geographic/Collection of the Supreme Court of the United States; pp. 40, 42 Library of Congress, Manuscript Division; p. 41 © Corbis; p. 43 Copyright © 1966 by the New York Times Co., reprinted by permission; p. 53 Arizona Historical Society, Tucson.

Designer: Evelyn Horovicz; Editor: Christine Poolos; Photo Researcher: Amy Feinberg